The Sorrow of Architecture

D1592559

The Sorrow of Architecture

Poems by Liam Rector

Dragon Gate, Inc.
Port Townsend, Washington
1984

ACKNOWLEDGMENTS

Some of these poems appeared, sometimes in different versions, in the following magazines: *Aleph* ("The Carpenter"); *American Poetry Review* ("Passing Cards," "David's Rumor," "The Sorrow of Architecture"); *Antioch Review* ("This City"); *Black Box* (on tape: "The Carpenter," "The Weather Gallery"); *Cimarron Review* ("In Snow"); *Cream City Review* ("My Drink Is Interrupted," "What We'll Do"); *Dancy* ("Morphine"); *Invisible City* ("Driving November"); *kayak* ("Saxophone," "We Colored Your Leaving"); *New Boston Review* ("My Grandfather Always Promised Us," "Showing," "You Are Arriving"); *New Letters* ("Laurence Harvey"); *Paris Review* ("Edvard Munch," "An Origin of A-R-T," "When Down by Long Boy's Lane"); *Partisan Review* ("Where You Get Off"); *The Reaper* ("At the Eating," "The Boy in Baseball," "It's Perfect," "Staying Up for England," "Those Who Go"); and *Shenandoah* ("As with One Hand," "The Eventual Music").

"My Grandfather Always Promised Us" also appeared in *Yearbook of Magazine Verse* (Monitor Books, 1980). "The Eventual Music" and "The Weather Gallery" appeared in *The Poet Upstairs* (Washington Writers' Publishing House, 1979). "Apartment" appeared in *Positively Prince Street* (Irene Rouse Bookseller, 1979).

"David's Rumor," then titled "The Rumor," was read into the *Congressional Record* of Monday, February 28, 1983 (Legislative Day of Wednesday, February 23, 1983).

I would like to thank the editors of these magazines for their work. I'd also like to thank the National Endowment for the Arts for a 1980 fellowship which buoyed matters, and thanks to Polly and Rudd Fleming, James Haft, Judy Karasik, David St. John, and Jeanne and William Wray for all their help.

ISBN 0-937872-16-4
ISBN 0-937872-17-2 (paperback)
LC# 83-20685

FIRST PRINTING, 1984
9 8 7 6 5 4 3 2

Published by Dragon Gate, Inc., 508 Lincoln Street, Port Townsend, Washington 98368. All rights reserved.

for David Rector,
for Elizabeth Wray,
& for Mary

Contents

Four

One

Where is that country not like others?
DONALD JUSTICE

Those Who Go

for Weldon Kees

She stands staring into the new traffic,
wearing the coat she was given in England.
He pays the porter and their bags are shoved easily
into the taxi of the new town.

They go where the money is, the elegant money.
Counting his recent change, the porter recedes,
moving into the swarm of those who go.
She takes off her coat to accommodate the shift,
the entrance weather here. Here it is humid,
but they will not be here long.

At the home of old friends, in the room they are given,
she pulls off her T-shirt, the one from an island somewhere.
How they have learned to excite each other.
His pants leave him next, the ones he has lived in
for over six years; his clothes announcing always
to him, "You will not be here long."

How they have learned to calm each other in their travel.
She takes from her small suitcase the coffee
she has always carried with her, something
that has always gotten her going. His bourbon,
to slow him down a bit, he puts on the table,
the table apparently in need of repair.

It has always been like this with their going,
and tomorrow they'll be gone again. They won't stay
for the repair, the abiding of the table,
or those who gather daily around. Those who do stay

are dreamt sometimes by what they know of this going,
and often to their loss and excitement.

Many stay and gather over the calm excitement
of the repair, sometimes blaming those who go.
If none stayed, no repair. None going, no way
of knowing what is out there, waiting,
though many imagine much, alone in their room.
You lose much and many when you go, though you imagine

that it all gathers round. See how the two of them repair
to each other, dress, then eat with their friends.
The talk turns quickly to the voyage and the burden
of each; how easily desire has carried them all off.

The Weather Gallery

1

Modigliani's paintings are being shipped by train
from city to city. In the car behind the Modigliani
car, cattle are being shipped from city to city. In
the car behind the cow car, I am being shipped, and
likewise, from city to city. I have hopped the freight.
The great art works, the cows and I are being shipped.
It is night and it is cold. I have a body temperature,
the cows have their body temperature, the great works
of art, the Modiglianis, have the temperature of canvas
and paint and the frames have their temperature also. It
is different for all of us. My face is not smiling, I
cannot see the faces of the cows, and Modigliani faces
seldom smile. We are all on the same train. The cows
will be eaten, the Modigliani paintings will be carted
off to the gallery, and I will eat as soon as we stop.
It is cold here. We are all on the same train.

2

I am at the gallery, having just been fed. The paintings, the Modiglianis, are unpacked and hung and indeed,
no faces smile. The cows are in some ways gone. A
piece of one of them is being digested somewhere
inside me, here inside the gallery. The temperature
has changed. I am warm.

3

The guard at the gallery joins our procession. He
appears in the gallery. I ask him what the great works
of art, the Modiglianis, mean to him. Are they more
than hats hung on a wall? "What's wrong with hats
on a wall?" he says. We let the thing rest.

4

My business is finished in the city. I hop the train
out. I notice there is a Modigliani car up towards
the front. I move to the corner of my car, talk
to my self about art. In the next city we will stop for
cows.

Passing Cards

This traveler steadies her sweaty existential palms
on the train where so much is obviously passing
by taking up the florid cards of solitaire,
a deep hand of solitaire.

She hears at once a remembered oboe and the horror
of the near-future in which she will have
no choice. She is running
out of money. The conductor extols the virtues
of free enterprise while the developing countries
erupt under her skirt. Like the cards that she holds,
much of what she sees is colored by chance
and power, and dazzles her.

She is off to some new place—she passes
her old home where her relatives applaud
her new life, the one they have seen on television.
She slips a black jack under a red queen
and the man across from her waves goodbye
to his old wife. There is a tendency,
she has noted, for the women her age to begin
to be kept by the older men who have not begun
to "face up to it." In faraway Africa
a "native" drinks his first Coke and waits for the effect.

She is not yet and no longer, between and distant.
How much farther, she thinks as she loses many hands.
How much farther, mother, the money in our hands?

The Eventual Music

for David St. John

Eventually someone knocks at your door eventually
just as the moon is eventual and just
as you were thinking that the only trust
is the trust of meat, the shift of need
and eventually someone knocks and you stand
at your own door   and you know then
that you are the door-opener and that someone
will enter, and someone does   and you tell someone
that you have been holding the world in its place,
in its place without music   you tell her
that fashion goes deep, fear goes deeper,
that you are intrigued by the chemistry
of what comes next   and someone eventually announces
that she is actually here and has arrived with music boxes,
tiny porcelain objects that never leave,
always stay and always music   she apologizes
for having come so late to your door   and you speak to her
of the bones that deny the music, of the arteries
and their race towards the skin, of the blood
that hears music always and eventually
runs away from home

and you lie down, with someone, in your opened door
and you hear all that music that was not there before.

My Grandfather Always Promised Us

The streets outside have ice on them.
On the nineteenth century farm where I grew up,
where my grandfather was a tenant farmer
for the old lady, her two mean dogs,
her large stone house and her constant small investments,
a cow slipped on the ice in those fields
and lost it, her life, though the cow inside her
was saved. My uncle and I fed the calf throughout
the entire winter, first with a bottle and then
from a gray pail, the milk of some other cow.
Where I live now
the old in the neighborhood are having their hard time;
the ice outside is hard for them.

Dogs blast at their heels, the wind chill
doesn't quite excite the blood that is already
slowing down and tired of running to catch them,
the ice seems to go on forever and the weather
stays where it is, everywhere. The old
have the absurdity of cows on these streets,
the grazing absurdity of cows. The young look
like dogs, the homeowners like wolves,
the sky itself so many nomadic animals,
clouded and quiet. Whether it's the field or the street
that gets us, I couldn't
say—but I can see my grandfather
moving towards the barn through perfect ice,
while the fields of his century move far,
and then farther away.

Showing

They showed up for awhile and they died.
They showed up for some while and they died.
They smoked a few cigarettes and were remembered
by others who showed up and died.
They played the piano; they sat reading.
They had dinner and went to the ocean.
They stared into the hospital they were born into
and they died. They remembered
years which were lost to them
unless they concentrated and they died.
All their fear died. All that concern over death
died for a moment and they died. All their curly hair
and the wide sky and their many walks shot up
into a memory remembered
by others who died.
All their photographs and their staring curiosity,
all their wake up and lie down, died. I knock
twice on your door, old boy.

Edvard Munch

for Jordan Smith

Eddie, you said you forgot about insanity and death
when you were at the beach. *From Beer to Eternity*
was as serious as you could take it.
"The land is holy" was as close as you came
to *Melancholy*. It changed you at the beach, Eddie—

        no talk of your mother's nightmares
        being family furniture   no talk
        of the stupor that finally broke your heart
        into activity   none of the
        "lick my sick prick quick"
        that made all your women orange
        and schizophrenic.

        Lots of talk, Eddie.

        No, at the beach you were different.
        Hart Crane hadn't yet leapt in an overcoat
        towards Caribbean love,
        but nonetheless, you
        made your "meek adjustment."

        At the beach, Eddie,
        you worried about your weight
        with the best of them. Your vanity
        waxed cultural and you were cheerfully
        embarrassed

and we all embarrassed each other that summer, Eddie.
The regrets that sprung from my hangovers
embarrassed us all.
You said "disease, insanity, and death"

were all absorbed by the larger family

here at the beach. You said
there was no need to worry
    and we went to the movies.

    Eddie, Hedy Lamarr was great in *Boomtown*—
    capitalism in its youth, Clark Gable
    at his height, Spencer Tracy,
    a *good guy*, licking his wounds
    in South America. . . .

    We practiced "the joy of submission," Eddie—
    all sun and only the work of recovery.
    You were wonderful that summer.
    We used to catch a light off each other
    before you returned

        and started that staring portrait
        with cigarette.

The Boy in Baseball

While you were considering the two hundred families with all
        the power
and yakking about the enemies of France, I suddenly
turned to the window now covered with frost
and began to make a sketch of the new impossibilities.

This sketch inadvertently reveals the boy in baseball,
he who drinks at a somewhat cheap though somehow
        charming tavern
near the stadium. He says that he has been married for
        thirteen years,
what he calls "thirteen long ones."

In this painfully telling yet commonplace scene
I hear you going on and on about the humiliation of
        the individual
caught in the "boss yes" and "boss no" of the industrial centers,
caught in what you are now calling a "managerial revolution."

I return to the frost for a moment and it seems clear
that the past does not occur *behind* the present, but is actually
quite far out to the front of it, and that whatever I think of this,
however nonsensical, is of little harm, and to be enjoyed as such.

You say that some "rough beast" is slouching towards somewhere
and that the truth is that no one is free enough to follow
        whatever meaning
all this might have. You note that someone recently smacked
        a minister in his eye,
someone who was tired of his turmoil, and that it took three
        weeks for the cornea to heal.

At this point my eyes have become so clear and blank that no sculptor
would try for them, and I'm thinking that I'll soon find my pockets,
the ones in which I shall place my hands for the eventual off-walking
I am soon to do, the solitude and shame of somehow leaving you.

You nervously implore me to fetch your pills and you mention
your long-chronicled involvement with what you accurately term
"the absinthe harbor of neglect," and as I view the details of
                your prescription,
upon returning, I note that you might somehow have pledged
                yourself to a more elegant calligraphy.

I learned from the lost drawings that the truest line finds itself
by going ahead and getting out there, fully into the emptiness,
and that emptiness has its own way of going. As we leave,
you nervously break down, in the old-fashioned manner
                of the 1950's.

I had meant to tell you that the boy in baseball had mentioned
                your name,
had recalled "a few brief moments" wherein your clothes had come off
like some awkward history that you were just then slipping out of,
and that he remembered you this way, indeed foretold you, impossible.

All this reminds me that people are finally silly and not enough
                like birds.
For the moment, let's make it home. It's true, the grains scream
                at the end of summer—
they're far from the beach and about to be cut—they know it,
                we know it—
we know, like the scorpion, that there is a deadening corner and
                of course, the sting of staying even.

In the car you are still grumbling about the boy in baseball—
            his hairy chest,
his perfect shadow. You say that he was just another "bullshit artist"
who never learned to work with his hands, that his eloquence is
            simply another quiz show, sponsored by noise.

You won't let the thing go about the boy in baseball.
I won't turn the wipers on, to rid the windshield of its frost.

Driving November

We are driving November we turned
October several towns back. We applaud
the passing of all that is innocent we inherit
the road as it is here. You speak of habit
as if things do not change I speak
of sweet repetition. We are driving November, from harm.

      And this, no actual car
      and out there, no eventual town

      The entire hospital shuts down

      A wheelchaired old man tosses paint
      on a canvas   A Great Dane
      gnaws on a beer can   We pass
      in the passing lane   An old woman
      passes out in the supermarket.
      In her funeral home she is dressed
      like a worker, embalmed
      by the night shift.

      The entire hospital

      We stop at a diner outside of town
      We take in the ceremony of knives and forks,
      the tenacity of salad and the fresh boredom
      of water   I learned to use a knife

at this table   In the thirteenth
century most of the vegetables
were fed to the sow   In three million years
we accumulated quite a list of meats   Mostly meats
with brains smaller than our own   We base our findings
on flattened molars,   the chew.

You speak of innocence as harm
and recount the turns of October. "You turned
against me many years back." And do I speak?
The radio comes on as if to applaud
the romance of routine, the ballad of habit,
the "baby's done gone" we inherit.

We two singers at this one microphone

We pull into a new city   naive
and opaque   Here are parks made private
by winter cold   We pull over
to nap the museum
"nothing personal" in these expensive rooms.
The GI Bill permitted many of the boys to study A-R-T

"He studied Marxism and poetry"

Dachau Dachau
If I knew how
I would leave now

We are dreamt as soon as we speak.
There are songs that we seem to inherit
on this road that we seem to applaud.
You continue to be dreamt by harm
until the breath of choice turns
you   (in all its syllables)   somewhere far from habit.

We sleep it off here   We sleep it on and off here
(Take your clothes off Johnny, it's time for bedlam)

Those who counted the money were off   Way off

The entire hospital shuts down

We carry our innocence
in a small paper bag   lunching
on the wheat of the past   We sit quietly
in the middle of each room as memory
commits itself to imagination   We take off
the clothes   the ones we could not afford

Let dog be dog

Buddha Bad Boys, early princes, the tense
goddess in her lonely green room—
Whorehouse Harry, Good Time Charlie,
the girl who smiles as she worries over nothing.

We peer into the loping mystery of dog
Let dog be dog

Dachau Dachau
If I knew how
I would leave now

Violent realism, plain fact.
The low-down humidity, all those Southern movies.
That still jar left standing in all of Tennessee.
Degraded kings who rule over their own misery.
The late summer of all our deals—Kafka cops,
shit chutes,   the keeping of wits.
"In the theatre, One is never alone."

The good animal, the great lyrical stone

"Could you put out that cigarette"

"No—am more attached to the cigarette
        than I am to you"

We drive to where the wheels are made.

The ones that take us.

Long, dusty highways   inherit—
I send you this letter   your harm.
You wear it well   your habit;
your hair beside me as it turned
long and long we've been turning, applaud.
This applause turns to memory to speak—

We hear all our schools   the "up and at 'em" Rimbaud school
the "when yr hot yr hot" school
the vo-tech school   the dubious art school
the kick-shit, fuck-you I-need-a-job school
the delicate, precious "have a look at my little poem" school

the concrete school   the stay cool I'll-risk-the-fool school
the where-did-you-get-schooled?
North of Nowhere   South of the Heat Wave
the "sinning with Annie" school

Our fears are blue ones

We didn't remain there the entire year. Odd jobs.
Live fast, die young.   Many pass.

You and I have dreamt November, from harm.

I roll down this window you see
I vote you this blue hello.

Two

Often at night I dream I can
No longer earn my living.

BERTOLT BRECHT

David's Rumor

for Dave Wale

I am busy doing drawings
    for the upcoming publication
Drawings of Schizophrenics in Closed Institutions.
I am busy doing drawings
    for the upcoming publication
Drawings of Schizophrenics in Closed Institutions
    because angelic voices will sing
    if I draw lost enough to listen

      and because it quiets the doctors down
      since they are anxious
      to see the book published
      and to have my efforts included. . . .

If I could find the right line, I could balance my entire design.

      Not everyone has a career,
      but the doctors have one, each of them,
      and the publication of the book *should* help to secure

      that section of their lives.

Alice, across the hall, is doing
a goodbye drawing. The doctors
are wary of this impulse
on her part, noting that Alice
says goodbye
too often. They encourage her to talk
of her plans, should she be released,
or of her past,
should she end up staying.

Alice tells them it's a "picnic,
a picnic in a light drizzle."

Here in the hospital Alice,
who killed Frank, crosses the hall each night
into my doorway and says,
"Frank, is that *you*, Frank?"

> In my drawings I omit Alice
> and concentrate
> on calling forth the hall. Schizophrenia,
> in this book, is another way of saying
> *across the hall.*

In the public room, the section where we sit and watch,
some read the newspaper while getting
the national news off the tube.
That way, if you read and listen,
you get the feeling
that the news is really coming at you,
that it might finally amount to something.

Of late I have begun to think,
I get the impression,
that our lives are being moved
by some very public rumor.

We, in darkness, picture ourselves alone
with some sort of headline: *Man Claims He Got Away
with Murder*, that sort of thing. . . .
We read as if dreaming and are then
dreamt as if living. Between

the solitary and the public, the rumor.
We picture ourselves closed-in, whirring,

but I doubt that.

In the drawings I stress
(and then surrender to) the fact
that there is some very 'hard news'
in all of us, a murderer
for each of us, and that this is how
all these reports, these *mayhems*,
finally do manage to reach us.

Pavese, the Italian, said that each
murderer is a timid suicide. Alice,
who killed Frank, wanders each night
for all of us, wondering who Frank
really is.

If I could find the right line, I could balance my entire design.

George, who lost his mind after losing
Carol, lives far down the hall. George says
Carol's infidelities at first made him want
to do away with himself, to surrender, but that later,
through the help of the doctors,
he realized it was Carol
that he wanted to kill
all along, that his impotence
was caused by a gun
that he didn't want to point

towards her, a thing he didn't want to see
go off.

None of this surprises me.
The drawings get so lost because the hall
is so wide. You come through a cauldron
before you ever sight home. . . .

My own crime bears no mention.
It was an argument, a debate gone wrong,
an affection historied into the berserk.

My work here now, my *calling*,
is to get these lines down right, to *delineate*
their deep gossip, that precise chamber
where they, right or wrong, do yak sublime. . . .

    And the doctors,
    the doctors say the book will receive
    national distribution and I'm glad,
    yes glad with all my heart,
    for that. Ambition,
    which is finally what we do to each other,
    will undoubtedly see this project
    into its rise and quiet. . . .

And the lines go off, they wander. . . .

If I could find the right line, it could balance, balance
this riot, that hall, that vacancy and pressure
wherein we draw towards goodbye.

The Carpenter

We never come to thoughts. They come to us.
MARTIN HEIDEGGER

Dwelling

    in

dimension
of floor.
Suddenly floor
is room. Room enough
here   now
Dwelling

as if dimension
were near and sudden.
As if
    taking measure.

Rector, get your ass going—
the pieces, measured and cut—the house, Rector,
the house.

Dwelling is residence is dimension

Alright Rector, don't get excited.
  Hold the hammer steady.

    Remember the terms, Rector—the terms.

    When I ask
        for a bastard file,

            when I ask you for a bastard,
            don't bring over one of your
            buddies.

        You got it made, Rector!
        You got it made

Measures are all
All around   There are bosses
                and Rectors. All this can be
                measured.   Marx, Feudalism,
                Studs Terkel.   Interviews of labor,
                laborers laboring to explain.   This
                is a sort of measure

                              taking place
                in a sort of dimension.

The boss must practice
self/concealment in order
   not to be
   measured.   Otherwise,
   maybe revolution.

   (Also motion in dwelling)

Rector, we get this fucking house built,
we're going out and tie one on—
You know Rector, you catch on quick
once you got the terms down.

Appearance must be mosaic,
          must be of a many dimension.
          Otherwise too little truth.
          Anger. Revolution.

You know Rector, it appears to me

       if I put you in a cage and made you
       lap up water, bent over and lapping out of a bowl
       with your tongue, like a dog, your only gripe
       would be about the cage. Now, I accept
       that there's cages around all of us—really
       Rector, cages! But I'll be damned if I'll lap

up water for any fucking bastard. Now why
don't that seem to bother you none, Rector?

The Brahman begs with a bowl, is fed
by bowl. The river knows where
it wants. The ocean is less certain.

Stay with the thinking
that the language itself does.
The power of this solitude is in many

dimensions. It can say

both *love* and *no more.*

The thought

of gathering falls

into oblivion in the face of

dimension.

Hey Rector—you know sometimes you're so quiet
it seems like you're my boss—
Listen Rector, I never asked for this job,
or any of this.

In the woods, along a road,
before a foot or a city or a need

    for that road began,
             there was something to be heard
             on that road.

             And this is not puzzle nor paradox,
             not story nor a moral, simply

             recall and road.

The thought recalls itself on this road.

Rector, I'm buying some land soon, you hear.
I gotta get away—got to—I wasn't meant to be
your boss, Rector—we should be partners.
Maybe someday I'll own my own business.

The weather changes on this road but the road is never
more nasty than you can stand. There is joy here and there is much
of what is other than joy. If you came looking for characters
there are characters here too. To be named they must be known.
One must have lived in the words one uses

or there is no road. In between this knowing and saying
is language.   There is much error
but then these are great games.   A blurring
of win or loss.   No sports page here.

Rector, I don't know what to tell my children you know,
the things we talk about   I, I can't seem to get it across,
stuff like that   I can't seem to get it across to them.
The most I can do maybe is teach them to be a carpenter,
which is what I learned.

The slow rattle of the chair when rising.

   Getting up.   The chair,

      what the carpenter said.
      In this room, many dimensions.

*You know Rector, I cut wood when I was a kid. Used to feel
like I was yanking those roots out, the way I cut. I felt terrible
about building as long as I was yanking. And they was being
yanked so's something could be built. Why hell, we made
our furniture that way.*

As long as it was origin it was endless

*I tell you, I get into a snarl every time I think of the past.
No real relief when there's so many ways of looking
at it. I tell you Rector, there's no chance for truth—*

there's too many of them.

As if it were near and sudden

    the chairs rock
    when left.

This much was said between us,

      rocking.

Apartment

I walk into apartment. The rooms
have been conversing. The kitchen
has been fuming and making loud accusations. The oven
with its stale breath, the sink
in its stupor, the indifferent
refrigerator. The bathroom
humming, as if it didn't notice
the bedroom which has been groaning
and lying on its stomach.

I walk further down apartment.
I am not one to interrupt   a conversation.

The oven door begins its flap and odor. It accuses
the United States of Hiroshima while the sink insists
it must go to the country soon. "My health,
my health." The floor is recovering from a drunk
in which it saw itself changing. The ceiling sulks,
jealous over nothing.

I sit in the small room of apartment.
The chair is tired; it complains of the light.
Only the windows laugh, and they laugh too much.

I cannot afford this place.
The bill for the rent slides in under the door.
It grins and lights a cigarette.
This must be part of the glamor of Manhattan,
what I came for—
the animate detail of price.

Where You Get Off

The reality of the building lies in the space inside it.
FRANK LLOYD WRIGHT

And where do you get off, calling me the Hyacinth Girl? Your taken apartment is burning; you worry what you will inherit. I send all my funds to apartment. Your "career" has turned banal; your apartment is burning. You smoked your first cigarette in condemned building.

Your earliest sorrow is building. The mood of your building is burning. That girl in your building is burning—the mood you inherit is ashen, and somehow the building is banal. Best now to straighten apartment.

We laughed when you first took apartment— we could see that it meant you were building. With your feet off the ground you were banal. And who is that girl that you built with? You inherit the mood that you're born with, burning.

Your first cigarette is still burning. You inherit it here in apartment—that ash that you burn and inherit—that smoke that now flies from your building—that air and that girl that you lived with—that girl that you burned with, banal.

The toast pops out, toasted banal. The electric that cooked it is burning. You breakfast with girl and with bacon—your apartment flies out of the building. Cruel gravity is what you inherit.

You always knew you'd inherit. She stares at you now, staring banal. She inherits the ground of your building—that girl stands apart now, burning. Partly what she said in apartment was that *she* was the Hyacinth Girl.

When born, you inherit what's burning. In this case, the banal apartment—the building you did with that girl.

It's Perfect

I don't think they should have separated
they looked so good together   of course
there are those who say "Well what difference does that make?"
and my only response to them is that something is making
a great deal of difference I mean look at it this way I've watched
the effects of looking good together in "my own life"
and I know it's certainly an abiding factor I picture
the old couple bony, skeletal in fact, clutching
each other's final cigarette-stained or passion-burnt fingers
perhaps in a tomb or say the tower of a metropolitan church
(Quasimodo and Esmerelda come immediately to mind)
and though of course Esmerelda never really went for Quasimodo
in the same fashion that she longed for Phoebus
the golden-haired warrior, the show-off,
readers and indeed filmgoers alike have for years now evidenced
the looking-good-together of wild, dancing Esmerelda, played
admirably by Gina Lollobrigida (who I understand
is keeping a low profile in Italy these days, surrounded
by trained dogs—she became wealthy over the years it seems
and is afraid of the rising new egalitarianism, what the dailies
call "the terror") with Anthony Quinn as her hunchbacked,
              oil-pouring
companion in seclusion, that obviously put-upon
              and self-parodying individual,
Quasimodo.   Earlier we saw a version
with Maureen O'Hara (with her fiery red hair in black
              and white) together
with Charles Laughton, who as it turns out was secretively
              homosexual.

Part of what goes on in this smoke-filled-club,
this meat shadow of costume drama, this nervous, flickering light
in which things bend, break, turn around or away, part of it
                        certainly
is *the way it looks together.*

Morphine

I see Eliot banking his way towards work
in the underground tube,
see his clothes, his hair, how it all suited him.
A "subtle conformist," Williams called him.
He sees currency moving in utter stillness—
I hear him saying *It is not a problem to be solved*
and living with it. In Boston
my best friend, my memory of him, measures
the Numorphan in the void
of his cleaned-again needle.
"It's synthetic morphine," he says. "Here they call it
new blues." He draws the blood
up into the new blue, boots it a few times,
lets himself have it, then sinks back,   mated
for the night   Mississippi still has
half-moons
on the doors of its motels by the bay.

Saxophone

Not by money—
MARKANTHONY MASTRO

When younger, money for pleasure.
Older, money that creates money.
Oldest, money for medicine, protection
from the elements that have become
the elements of money.

Pleasure, protection,
Guilt money, gold the color of wheat
grown on "real estate,"
Farm money, Wage Earners, their "careers,"
their cities, Car money for the suburbs,
subways to bring them in for their money,
Bank money, trust, savings, standing in line
for Cash money, Coin money for the machines
to wash the Clothes money, Laundered money,
Drug money, the sons and daughters
of Economists' money, Boat, Plane and Get Away
money, The Arts money, I-Love-You-Honey money
for the dinners whose table and atmosphere
are the discreet sauce of Food money,
my money, your money, our "tax" money,
Pound's money, money for an ounce, a half-gallon,
a fifth, Milk money, money for the containers
containing the distribution of money.

Promotion money, earning "good money,"
having no money, doing it for money.
Money turned to power no longer
money, money through time, the spirit
of money—secular, psychological money.

Who's Got and Where Can We Get
some money?

You and I, our money. Their money.
Our pleasure and fist full of money.
Laughter over money, serious laughter
over money. Too much, too little,
fluid money. The saxophone, color of wheat,
purchased through Hock Shop money, saxophone
splitting the night, our air, blowing money.

This City

for Bertolt Brecht

This apartment with no furniture,
where no one puts anything up,
where everyone schemes to get out.

This mess, to the right and the left of me,
that equation of garbage wherein matter moves its way,
the magazine sector in glanced-at demise.

This price, and that mind, and nothing to say but "violent."
Nothing but violence in the expensive mind.
Moving from the window towards morning.

These characters at the bottom, so generous
and pathetic. Those abstract things at the top,
so mean, precise and arresting.

That god-abandoned theatre with its three-legged dog.
Staying alone to learn the lesson, the lesson being
DO NOT SPEND NIGHTS ALONE FOR AWHILE.

This program, these organizations, these gatherings
and awards. This sweat that drags it down.
These pagans with large teeth and good eyes.

The profit sector giving us images, the nonprofit
passing out handbills, and worried.
The mind that grabs after information.

The dance changed every week so no one masters
any one dance. Carrying around the little guns
and knives, the bars owned by a friend.

The same economy that binds them together
pulls them apart. The little thems, staring
into the canyon. The all of us.

A sense of proportion, in this dense heat,
hearing the tune of romance behind the psychotic.
The profit sector giving us images.

Elegance, learning, poverty and crime.
Those who smell power must dog these.
The untuning of cement into many moods.

In audacity, in hilarity, this city
plays an unbelievable organ.
How afternoon goes like the movies.

Three

The detail of the pattern is movement . . .
T. S. ELIOT

An Origin of A-R-T

Winsome Bob meets Katherine and drops Nancy.
Nancy burrows even deeper
into her studies of semiology, at Yale.
Bob, following his penis
after languid years of domestic affection,
goes to Ann Arbor to join Katherine,
who fitfully jabs at her doctorate
concerning the History of Art.

Bob takes up Arts Administration at U. Michigan,
picturing a foothold
into the world of money and aesthetics
for Katherine and himself.
Meanwhile Nancy drops her studies (at Yale)
and flees to the opposite coast, to read.

As is often the case between money and aesthetics, matters
between Katherine and Bob
grow extremely problematic and full of accusation.
Bob, about to hit 30 and tired of life
not seeming as lyrical as it is rumored to be,
dashes off a whining epistle to Nancy,
to her sad end of the continent,
to which he scampers

after discussing things with Katherine,
hedging his bet by leading Katherine to imagine
that he may someday return to Ann Arbor,
their Arts Dream still intact, and he ready to move

on it, possessed then by an unusual clarity of mind
and a thoroughly winnowed-out sense of purpose.

Nancy, by now, has been
in the Bay Area for over 7 months,
recovering her love for the great books
and the solitude out of which great love
has always grown.
"No fire" is all she has for Bob
after the attempted reconciliation,
the shore lapping at their feet and so on. . . .

Calling Katherine in Ann Arbor, Bob discovers Katherine
wants no more of the lad,
that she has met a Transportation Consultant
in whom she is vaguely interested.
Bob, losing all aplomb
and sensing the criminal in himself for the first time,
accepts a hefty fellowship
from the University of Massachusetts

where he vows to recount this tale
in all its brutal animation, honing in
on how static it all seemed as a narrative event
but how many moves, how many telling details,
how much inordinate sorrow
it actually involved.

Until There Is Something

I had money and I didn't care
and it was warm and I had as long
as I needed to get where I was going
and there were no rides on the highway

and I napped in a ditch,
in the long golden grass of a ditch.
The next day I passed through a small town
and for a dollar I was let in

for a double feature and I slumped back
and sucked at its drama.
That evening I met a woman
who took me in and told me

her past was so bitter she needed
"something to look forward to"
and then I was on her, then in her,
and then I told her

she was "really something" and not
to worry, but to wait, tossing the bitter
above her, and days later,
when she was back on her feet

and I back to the highway, I passed
an astonishing night,
and trusted desire to separate us
as it was desire which brought us,

and was lifted away from the one I'd left
in the first place, knowing no matter
(that voice which offers, in healing,
"never mind") what turned round to end us

there would be nothing now
for many a moon,
knowing the moon then
as it planted each dry slip of grass

I had come to depend on, knowing
the highway with its vengeance
not unlike my own, one I could abide with,
flickered into the long hours of nothing

because I had money and didn't care,
because I heard then the prayer, my murmur
to the matinee, to the hysterical hours
I would sit with, recalling her, seeing myself

waving, turning back and waving
through the long grass of memory where I go now
to meet her.

In Snow

With the window sitting with you,
and with glass, with air to see with,
there I came with you to be with,
asking *if* and *ever were*.

And with snow, with wet and moving,
there we brought the afternoon in.
Soon with gin we poured the ache down
and with window sitting with us

soon we felt the air we moved with.
Now in snow and later raining
we went out and moved the walking
and in snow resumed the drifting

of the past that we'd been speaking.
I was cold and you were raining—
I had stayed while you went leaving
and the life that I was walking

turned to air, and then went dark.
You now mentioned all your leaving
(now that afternoon had left us)
and you rained with need and grieving

for that staring boy you'd left.
I recalled the boy who saw you
as you moved through girl, through bleeding,
and I mentioned movement boyward

where in snow we'd lain all needing.
We lie down, within this window,
and in snow, in rain and moving,
we give back our time its longing

over field and snow and leaving.

We Colored Your Leaving

We colored your leaving this way—

    those who had been nowhere called it
    the blank white of going
    and stayed with their stare.

    Those who closed their eyes and saw other places
    called it the red wish to return,
    the long whine of memory as it arcs into action.

    Those who had been and returned
    saw something dark, silly in the going,
    calling you

    the dupe of friendship, the fool of love.

When Down by Long Boy's Lane
a ballad for the old boy

A visionary bowler,
gone down by Long Boy's Lane,
a casually bitter stroller,
a roller with the strain,

went dancing dark through night-town
(suggesting day was done),
fell flat onto the sidewalk
hardly lost but barely won.

The night was to the bowler
as pig is to the ham—
the inside/out of bowler,
the darkness in his hand.

The bowler wanted sky-town;
he stepped into the bars.
He felt the night crawl into him
and dreamt the dreaming stars.

The bowler thought of lovely hair,
of hair in which he cried.
His eyes could see the perfect air—
that air that moves the sky.

The bowler's drunken sun-up,
the sky with perfect rain—
the bowler grips his planet,
this bowler's earthly lane.

If gods sing to the bowler,
they toast a bitter cup.
When he is looking down from stars
they tell him to look up.

The moonlight, often striking,
as down by Long Boy's Lane,
the bowler drinks the morning
with vision, and in rain.

As with One Hand

As two blind men wave goodbye to each other
as each with his dog, one the train out,
the other taxi home. As four women settle
at a table laughing at the air, the air
invisible, air intimate with everything.

As with the dog and the distance filmed
through dust which scratches the camera
and its gaudy claims on realism tonight
as on a boat as a cut that will not stop bleeding
to death as we all are, buoyant, tentative, going

as the oar places itself in the water while with one hand
the shore changes all about us tonight
where a dog waits on the shore and cannot see us,
the dog that we are as tonight
the small boat which brought us out here

crashes against wharf, our small boat.

My Drink Is Interrupted
for James Haft

They are crossing the border and I witness
their crossing. I ask them
what sort of frontier they had in mind,
what sort of currency they brought with them.
There is, of course, the question of how they look
and the effect this will have on their crossing.
They are not old enough to have gotten the faces
they will eventually deserve, but I look anyway.

A hellish gang of street birds crosses the border
following the weather in their sky. We cannot see
the faces of birds at this distance, cannot tell
what they are facing. Our attention, our sky swerves,
falls, undoes itself, loops, careens and wavers
for a moment and of course, the machine of interrogation
shuts down. But I pick it up again.
At this distance I have learned
to pick it all up again.
I look. Look.

Obviously some sort of birds are flying somewhere.

These two are anxious to cross the border and that much
seems obvious. I could stop them
here, the way I have stopped others.
I have my doubts.
I look to the hills which have ceased
to travel, and to the clouds, still
traveling. At this distance
to merely drink from a glass
would change everything.
To recall those birds

(they of course were calling and calling)
would be to have somehow crossed.
Anything mere can do it, and at any time.

They pick up the luggage.
I shrug and instruct them to pass.
They accept the affection in this gesture
and they make their crossing.

One of them looks back and says,
"I also have my doubts."

I am glad to hear this.
I have been here for months.
It's getting so I can tell
who is going to cross over.

I return to the long drink I am taking,
the bird crossing.

You Are Arriving

You are passing through customs
with your portable museum, your old umbrella,
your trigger-happy extroversion.
Your museum includes many
a wide-eyed American, vulgar yet curious,
clothed in ill-fitting pants and expensive
shoes. Your umbrella features
the rain of Seattle, sun over the Algerian coast,
smacking the hell out of someone on the street.

The natives grow restless in your museum.
You tell them to calm down, that you are entering
yet another country. You tell them they are robbing you
of arrival, that you meant to be out and going.
These tiny figures
complain of the demise of the dollar,
the cold food and the foreign arrogance.
They threaten
to expose your ruthless carnival,
to the proper authorities.

A uniform steps up to inspect your goods.
He shakes the weather from your umbrella
and you quiet down.

He says simply, "We are always with you . . .
                        today in paradise . . ." and so on.

You decide there's no use in going

and you settle somewhere near the woods
with your tiny colony.

Taking off your stockings
after a hard day on your legs, you murmur,
"The open spaces, my umbrella, so much
for the inner life."

At the Eating

I was waiting for them
when they finally came back
appearing through the humidity.

I had been waiting by the back door
by the screen door
of our very large kitchen.

They had walked into villages
alone and that was all on their faces
those faces I had waited for

staying here, at a terrible job,
reading newspapers I never cared for
in our very large kitchen.

They had thought about me, told
the villages about me, had come back early
since they knew I was waiting.

We sat on the white porch
and watched the getting-dark drama
of the streets that were still and expiring and

we got into a toy car, moved only by a slight hope,
and passed quickly to those villages
where they were waiting, a spoon for each, and eating.

Staying Up for England

Once I lived in the Visionary City
among Visionary Company and the rest of it

before this dizziness set in, this panorama
of Teeth-Showing Doubt coupled with Epic Ambition,
this marriage of the impossible and the unlikely.
When these two get together they argue all night

and I hear all of it.
I listen to them as if they were animals,
as if I were not. I think they are both
wrong I wish they would move away.
I think of sending them to Florida.
My own youthful retirement is sending me
to England and I don't want these two keeping me awake
in the nights before I leave   I stay up and doubt.
It's true that doubt is intelligent and means
to have its way. It means to cancel out.
And ambition, if it involves itself with ethics
at all, doesn't really want any friends.

So I stay up and audience their chatter.
Someone out there is starving.
Perhaps I should go sit with them.
Perhaps I am proving some sort of God
with this wide-eyed exhaustion. Who knows?
And furthermore, who proves?

I don't know; I don't.
I'm going to England.

I heard a lecture somewhere
about memory, about how memory
runs throughout the body, is even
in the knees, the ankles, contained
in runners called *engrams*. Engrams have the sound
that is moving somewhere
though the neighborhood and its cars
are grazing fast asleep, their lights out and gone....
Some sort of dance stays up to stay
with it, a dance where more knees are needed
for the quick turns, the swerve
that delivers the present
and all its foretelling....

I don't know; I don't.
It's England where I'm going.

I left my keys there.

The ambition says, "I am the memory that will rut your face,
                    the present tense that races you
                    from place to place."

The doubt says, "Lie down and I will cover you."

Laurence Harvey

We seem to be in some sort of British car
wherein you are wealthy and broken down,
I apparently your chauffeur and teeming
with sexual energy. You ask me,
quite innocently, what the prevailing passions
of my life have been. I point to the sadism
of my early youth, the constant fighting
in the "inner city," my own romantic sense
of some "other shore," and my eventual flight
to the English countryside.

You ask me, a bit anxiously, if I can do something
about your headache, your disappointment, your child
who died early in a gaping car-wreck. I can't.
You ask me how I came upon my present hardiness,
my cheerful indifference,
my not giving a shit
about the economic disparity that now characterizes
our journey. You climb over the seat.
I inquire about your husband, his habits,
his holdings and your discretion. You report
that you had been handed over at an early age,
an ignorant age, and that your life has not been
your own.

We're getting along well here in the country.
Some locals standing by a lake wave us on.
They suspect we're some idiots from London,
perhaps touring some investment. Crudely,

a bull climbs the rear of some cow in a distant field.
You're still wondering about your life, its way of going.

"You let yourself go and you go," my stout father once told me
and you can't.

We were talking about the weather, how it changes us. Talking about weather in the cities. Talking of whether we should go or stay. We decide that the sky is our certain weather, and that it is weather that we need. And that the stars are the end of a long day of weather. It occurs to us that afternoon is some of the best weather and we begin to see all our cities on this afternoon in rain.

We have been talking since the weather changed. You suggest Seattle and suddenly I think of Kansas City, quiet rent, an equation that is canceled in its own equality. London is brought up and the possibility that we could gain employment as American readers with an ear for "hysterics." I am thinking of New York again—how I should return and slay the dragon. You mention Northern California and the great fact that we fucked there for months on end. You say that we could be pulled again by that same damp gravity.

Already I'm thinking of Massachusetts, how they know how to live there. I'm thinking of Lenin's dictum about "plain living and high thinking." How much those people know about shoes and how to live that weather. How I could learn to dress there.

We're going on and on about weather. You say that we should forget about the Plains, that you are tired of so much red dirt. You seem sure that we should know the score by now. We let go of "experience" and the subject changes to our love for our friends —anyone we could save with our travel? You speak of the one who has begun to answer the phone, long distance, drunk and bitter. It seems to us that this might signal deterioration. It seems that we should stop by, that the pressure is rising.

We talk of the rain in the smaller towns and the mean annual runoff of the younger people there, the shallow depression of the land in certain spots, and how this affects us all. The rapid fall of rain in those towns does little to change us.

It seems that bad weather has always brought with it some sort of sudden change, and that this is a rain that will not be over in the next few minutes.

If the wind stays up, we will go on talking. We associate this with no immediate change. The sky darkens under wide stars. We call all our friends and discuss this with them. We know that the weather is with us, and that this is what we will do.

Four

What falls away is always. And is near.
THEODORE ROETHKE

The Sorrow of Architecture

Out of the building, out of the buildings the great sorrow
of not knowing what to do
pours; the great movement of not knowing
where to go, goes. By the hour
it has been moving towards this;
the snow which fell for an hour
reminded everyone of the suspension—
call it an *image* where the forgotten
is gazed at again, the long hour
of our marriage bringing us to this.
Out of the building
and all that leans back tomorrow failing
into the field, pours the sorrow
of going, the suspension
of gone. Look there—the quickly mentioned
divorce of a colleague and, leaving by herself,
a recent widow. The snow pounds its thorough white
all through the dark megadorm of the city
where we each widow-walk the nighttime air
by the river, outlived
by any embrace that might hold us, outsmarted
by the innocence that might send us home.

––––––––––––––––––

We go out one night, and you say that those you've lost
scar up buoyant in your sleep, that field
where the lantern insects of summer give everything up,
bowing to the frost and relief of all that stirs them
from underneath. From underneath

our bluest fear pivots, blasting through hope into notion,
grabbing at all that drowns away. In the afternoon
between-hour, or that other one at night,
doesn't everyone give them up? Most of what we mean to love
disappears during sleep, where you say each one wades
through many dreams alone, waking to live them
with the little they remember. You say that we lie down
finally in one vast sleep, in the many dreams, driven on
by the lovers, gaping into prebirth or breath-pleasure
in their looming house. We picture the dead
as we have lowered them into their field,
a retired office in a lull of light, living
in the manner that the building lives, holding
a puny and sublime suspension
as a sky carols on. No wonder
one of us once stared out far and called
the entire undertaking *impossible.*

Coming in for a moment, out of the cold,
we wonder if anything we have built is that thing
which will outlast the sorrow, the seeming
not to last. I doubt it. And you, who could never stand
a biting doubt as part of the diet, are already moving
in some other direction, eaten
by your indifference, your only hope.
These last few months have been waving
the entire thing away, and it gets down now
to the hours. I hear you talking in your sleep.
Will you not let it go, return to me? Can I count on you
to leave with that other man, the one you've met often
this winter, in the after-hour? The marriage
glides snout-down with you smelling of him, this close to me,

saying to yourself *I am back to myself again*
and to the rest, *Fuck it.*

––––––––––––   ––––––––––

When I tried to count an entire arc of stars,
as a child, I thought
I could always return to that impossible task,
as a rush-hour returns to an economy,
after sleep. We thought later we could lie down
thigh to wide-open, hair to hair
with others, in the deep breath and relief
of those many bodies and their stirring choice.

Sleeping with others . . . the night-sky widens
and the reference dims;
the light comes again and our count
is wiped away.

A wide sky is what we had in mind.
The arc is always the telling line,
the remark that floats up begging
its final scene.

––––––––––––––––––––––

Do you remember that film that ends
with Robert Mitchum calling Shirley MacLaine,

saying he is going back to where he came from,
that he doesn't know why exactly but he is going back?
MacLaine is sitting in her small apartment,
trying to absorb
his leaving, and Mitchum is in the wide hall
of the place he will leave. The scene cuts
from one telephone to the other, until both places vanish
and there is only the voice, only what they want
and will not have. After that,
only turning out the lights, the hand that goes for the luggage,
and the one who goes. Or the staying,
and the staring, of the other.

———————————

The thing about architecture,
as you've said, is that there is no such thing.
The building vanishes back over that line
into prebirth, invisible, as a line glowing
in the mind passes to the pencil and the plan,
the blueprint of possibility and need.
The buildings lean into me
as I make it back out onto the streets,
walking the voice we once had for each other,
waiting its instruction.

You've stayed inside; you are tired of walking.
Your mother told you once
that marriage is in many ways putting one foot in front

of the other, sleep-walking through the dream of choice.
Yes, you're exhausted. Stay where you are.

I think I can hear it, what vanishes and is.
I step up to a public phone to call you and tell you.
The city slides back into the invisible,
impossible, and there is sorrow on the line.

Notes

In "Driving November," *Let dog be dog* is from *Three Antiphonies* (Proteus Press) by Carlo Parcelli; *Dachau, Dachau / If I knew how / I would leave now* is from a musical by Douglas Himelfarb; *Sinning with Annie* is the title of a novel by Paul Theroux (Houghton-Mifflin, 1972). Certain turns of phrase in "The Boy in Baseball" are occasioned by lines from the work of Robert Lowell.

The sources for epigraphs on section title pages are as follows:

"Where is that country not like others?" is from Donald Justice's poem, "A Sestina on Six Words by Weldon Kees."

The Brecht quotation is from his "Poems Belonging to a Reader for Those Who Live in Cities."

"The detail of the pattern is movement" is from Eliot's "Burnt Norton."

Roethke's line is from his poem "The Waking."

A Note on the Author

Liam Rector took his graduate degree from Johns Hopkins University and has taught at Goucher College, George Mason University and The Phillips Academy. He has also directed the poetry programs at the Folger Shakespeare Library in Washington, D.C., where he now lives with his wife Mary and daughter Virginia.

Rector, Liam, 1949–
    The sorrow of architecture.

    I. Title.
PS3568.E29S6   1983   813'.54   83-20685
ISBN 0-937872-16-4
ISBN 0-937872-17-2 (pbk.)